the vulture girl:
necessary and sufficient conditions

the vulture girl:
necessary and sufficient conditions

Carrie Nassif

SADDLE ROAD PRESS

Saddle Road Press
Ithaca, New York
saddleroadpress.com

Interior and cover design by Don Mitchell
Cover image by: Em and Carrie Nassif

ISBN 9798987954164
Library of Congress Control Number: 2023945935

Books by carrie nassif
lithopaedion

CONTENTS

twin

rabbit

old stag

little wing

vulture

fawn

tornado

twin

yesterday the gods told me to fall into my own eyes

to find my own frame to live each breath into the broken body
of the rabbit we hit on the dirt road

to inhabit her truths and translate the torn and
sinew and quick and gasping breaths

to recall
being prey

to stop the car to gently to cup her pain in my hands
the spare heft of her infant size

fur the color and soft of sifted dust
to set her to nestle under the grasses

to assign her a place safe from the gullies of tire treads
leave her looking up into the weeds

the green bounding arches into
the white spaces carved out around the trees

to set her deep into shade
the black of her eyes in shock

to witness her fleet and dance
drain inert

as if I were holding my vanishing twin
whom I can only assume I had interrupted

had just the same had run into
had collided had absorbed had invited within

would her cells retain the stamp of those urges or the caution
not to spring across the road in fear of barreling noises

a quiet wisdom within of one who had her fatal wounds
tended to who held my hand

as I became alone

I still keep my wisdom teeth and four bicuspids in a green jar

I wonder if my mother kept anything
besides her silence

any proof at all of the accusation
tell your sister, she was born a twin!

which she spat over her shoulder as she was walking away
the last thing she'd directed towards either of us

since declaring us dead to her
the first time

such a strange thing to tell my younger sister
such an odd thing to say

if it weren't true

Des Moines 1972

a toddler waits in tights with lace along the seat
where the red smocked dress and she both end

pudgy feet forced into stiff patent shoes
by a mother hard-pressed to bend down

due in two months with my sister her hair
a curtain of honey let loose from her ears

always something in the way

we become

as we split
nearly in half

cojoined in magnetic in
gravitational orbits

binary stars now
tumbling away from the other

seeds
we

g r o w
e x p o n e n t i a   l   l   y

in.a.finite

(space)

it is estimated that one out of every 3-5 single human births

were multiples at some point after conception at least according
to the internet where she does most   of her research   meaning

we literally *litter* *as in: an untidy collection as in: materials*
strewn about to absorb urine as in: trash as in: waste as in:

carry it away upon as in to fill with unpleasant examples
as in   bedding as in   a place to rest

twinning   she declares to herself   surely has to do with the
forces of natural selection and overproduction even in-utero

as it is for other mammals   but for centuries   people didn't
acknowledge couldn't have known didn't think to keep track

most of the time never even suspected how often this happened
in humans   especially back then   unless there had been an extra

heartbeat detected early on and lost unless there had been some
remains the *fetus papyraceous*   a flattened corpse

the birthmark on my left foot she kept trying to scrub off

rabbit

permeable membranes

learning you through osmosis /mother/ elbow-
grit and just so and all the bedtime-story voices

the harsh shove-your-nose-in-itness   a certain
stance   the pinch of fingernails   lift of one brow

it all gets passed down even past me to the one
I birthed and when I was in your womb I left the

residuals of my genetics there for you and for my
younger sister   too   there is evidence in cases of

mistaken identity or questions of paternity that find
traces of male DNA in the blood of mothers of sons

proving our braided entities   there can be
no washing our hands of each other   so easily

wall arrives too late

there is the everydayness of their leavings a liminal moment
when their everything   disintegrated into her nothing

into the girl who was left behind her bare feet on carpet
toe heel toe heel to make sure

there is the suck of the refrigerator seal opening
bland light scrubbing the dusk kitchen floor

empty stomach calculates risks of eating two pieces at most
of the cheap white bread a handful of macaroni and cheese

plucked cold from the uncovered casserole dish peels
off the crusts and smashes the insides into a tight ball

so that she would feel like something of substance
like the fat pizza box in the fridge still warm the smell

of thick crust so fresh it broke her

reckons she could eat one piece without it being missed
ate another this scrounging animal she had become

ate another ate another in the unlit apartment before bed
full belly slept so well even wall sleeps hard as rocks

until mother's red fingernails her red mouth her red howl
a shape of outrage even the girl hadn't seen before

cussing over stolen pizza pulls her into the kitchen pins
her head onto the almost empty box waxy with grease

fluorescent lights buzzing the girl is only ears and eyes
the mother is everywhere else   a fork in one hand the other

on the girl whose face is not holding the box on the countertop
anymore yelled at like a chain saw up close and too loud to hear

and there.is.then.there.is.just.the.flashing.of.the.fork and spit and
wadded bits of food speckling the wet floor and she is fighting

there is no air no sound at all underwater in the deep end
she was everything a mother was supposed to be somewhere

underneath and she and the fork it keeps and it keeps and she still
and it keeps

hypothetical twins and similar inner parts

to the kernels of her I may or may not
have wandering within me

I nod I extrapolate their presence
project them into my body as if

that were someplace else
other than me other than

us   their legs twitching in my sleep   like
specters of shaken snow-globe storms sealed

off & siphoned within fragile cell walls splitting
old fragments seeping out now secreting these

memories embedded just under my skin   like
slivers of glass finding their own way   to surface

we are ever always pale

pinched and clenched in pee-soaked bedding she
dreams of technicolor rectangles of billboards the

size of whole houses taking up the entire sky &
broadcasting neon colors of TV static   we push

pause
for her

and we
endure

mother this actual human

she took us to an almost empty beach had woken
us up early to go ratty terry cloth shorts and a thin

t-shirt over her old bikini tousled hair dark at the roots
split in two uneven braids   ivory skin and barely-there

freckles pale gray-green eyes softened   if only for
one quiet sunrise near a wild patch of weedy sand

in which I seek my guide

a shadow of a rabbit
shows me a burrow

that she's dug a feral
honeycomb   a nest

of the earth itself
lined with her fur

a refuge in my
very own belly

we have both made the best
she says   *of what we were*

of what we were given she
whispers   *come closer*

she gives my hand   a small
squeeze with her paw   *let*

me show you how   she
tutts   *to live in your guts*

in which she enters another rabbit hole online

and is charmed by the word *chirality*   its
design of reversely asymmetrical particles

discovers the building blocks of all of us
formed from comet dust   and radiation

the exposure left them circularly polarized
imprinted chemically   leaving a particular

ratio of leftward spinning molecules   to
rightward ones so every one of our cells

has a handedness   she imagines them
waving at each other in an infinity mirror

never quite touching
never quite   leaving

wonders if her twin would have been
right-handed had a cowlick that spun

an opposite swhorl on the other side
of the back of her head a mole on the

other edge of her mouth both of them
never quite dying   never quite living

spooky action at a distance

if you ask quantum physics   it will tell
you everything is just a matter of scale

it can't say exactly if   you and your
vanishing twin are entangled or not

but when particles share space in such a way
that they cannot be described independently

then observing   one
causes an irreversible

collapse within the other and I wonder
what is a collapse   without a hope for

consolidation
of the rubble

old stag

she first saw old stag several years before they'd met

in a gravel driveway she comes across a part of his carcass
can't look away can't keep looking without wonder

takes wide steps to greet him hovers a pulse and then plunks
down stiff knee and all to squat to peer closely this need to

witness skull to skull to claim   somehow   these
familiar remains among a stranger's weedy wind row trees

today she summons old stag's presence she unfolds
dog-eared pages of questions she kept she thanks him

for bearing what all she'll never know of \not now\ she searches
for words like *browse* and *forbs* and *hard and soft mast* instead

that he would have loved to have heard she draws evergreen
leaves and clover   chicory and vetch and buckwheat   oats

and alfalfa and rye

she gathers a great pile of last year's acorns and this year's early
summer seeds and berries in honor of him

of tonight's   post-solstice   strawberry   full   moon
she arranges them on a bed of mosses and mushrooms on stones

themselves quilted with ageless lichen in every possible form of
filament and pigment she makes a basket of her arms

the same shape they made circling around his neck when
he would stride her out to safety

she leans   she bows forward into the tender tang of the woods
her cheek on the soft nest of her offering

and folds over on her stomach the way she'd slept as a small girl
and wept   she wept   sweetly

when I tell you that our mother has always been a
force of nature

that is not to say
that the woman who carried us was a hurricane of intensity

although
she was

no
I mean that

we had turned to the moon for comfort
since very young

she was cold and stern
but always seemed to find us in the dark

so hard he dislocated his own shoulder

earliest memories   she
half-wakens to sobbing

goes hunting for the
animal sounds down

dark hallway's
wooden floors

clambers up her lap
damp with tears

stretches her arms
far around   as she

can   scolds her
grown-ups aren't

supposed to cry
as she rocks her

hearts beat
beatings

red-orange
lullabies

rabbit and I play hide and seek for years

I sense her in my body when I smell the claggy loam of dirt
ripe with mushrooms or the garlic tang of wild chives and

the licorice scent of purple basil   but mostly I
am too busy behind wall to notice body at all

somedays I borrow from her tensile strength
coiled up in our entrails   draw it from within

to the four corners of my heart   gently stretch
into the grace of her mottled grey hide we are

so used to stretching   this cartilage gives and
gives easy   it unwinds flexible from our navel

I step into the rabbit skin a thin layer just under mine
and her ribs grow to encase me and I expand toward

her and ask if I might rest in her space
which is really ours/mine   for a while

at the white house on Ingersoll

to the girl   the full moon was that pocket-watch
on a chain that mother wore

filigreed flowers   blooming like craters
blood   too magnetic to hold time against her

skin   she kept it layered
like sky   thropping now and then

against her   sternum
its shine too bright   to stay in

bed   the girl plods down the hall
toward   lamplight   haloing mother

to the reverent flow   of practiced hands her
rhythmic sewing   a tidal ritual   sign-language

spells cast in the mending the way
her threaded spirals part the air

the girl feels her own fingers twitch   her arms stretch
to rise   to trace   the ethereal magic   of mother's face

who recoils in disgust
at the unbidden touch

207 W Allen St

she's in that room in the old house with these same double
windows back when she snuck too much circle-cut fruit soaked all

day in a carved watermelon bowl on the kitchen counter before
the grown-up's party full of what she now understands was

sangria so sweet and sticky she hallucinated birds and monkeys
that night out of the macrame hung spider plants flying and

leaping across the room scaring the bejeezus out of her younger
sister back when they shared that lavender room one girl on each

of dad's childhood unbunked twins with hand-sewn quilts that
matched but she is in fourth grade now and as the oldest gets

first dibs to claim the room for herself   which she does because
she hates the color red   even if that forces her sister into the

basement room with its strawberry shortcake sheets to go with
the shag carpeting and immune to her meek sister's pleading and

begging so fearful of crickets and change and alone and eversince
then she has been in that square room looking out those double

windows at the greenish storm-at-sunset skies the darker grey of
cottonwood trees in the dusk the way they like two hands

clasp their whole selves around each other first surging west
then eastward like an argument between parents made of

bird-feathered trees she falls asleep to every night listening
for her own breath arranging her knees into a number 4

checking every so often that her star was still there in the other
the single window to her left just hidden by the pane

wait until your father comes home

and then she wouldn't speak to us
till he did   long weeks until he

got back from the road   he'd
holler to us   *get the stick*   &

whupt us   with all his 300 pounds
arm raised over and over &   we'd

scream and scream puffy red welts
and black bruises on the bare ends

of our backsides   *give me a hug*
he'd plead on one knee   when it

finally would stop

our ears still wrung with shock
this hurts me   he would coo

worse
than you

she tells herself she is digging for water

grandaddy longlegs had taken over the old play house
the tractor-tire full of sand more full of weeds and we

won't get let inside till lunch anyhow so hard at it
she digs for hours past the sand   digs all afternoon as

dirt gives way to clay until the worn shovel pries up
just shallow shavings and blisters always what next

being busy keeps wall strong and that was what wall wanted
more of this of seeing where you've been more sticktuitiveness

even at play at pretending to escape let's go let's go let's go
but if she could have tunnelled all the way through the earth

back then the way she wanted to we would have come out
in the middle of the Indian Ocean—she looked it up online

if she could have dug that hole all the way down
at that time   we all   would have drowned

as the part of her that never left Chickasaw County

imagine how to be one of a pair of girls how to be the daughters
of an exacting of an insecure mother how to reckon with a

charisma only you two could see through how to pry below her
diamond studded skin to find the hands that once shoveled pig

shit that collected chicken eggs eyes streaming the smell almost
a concussion just to look inside the henhouse never mind wade in

how the smell stains her school dress like onions having to wear
blue jeans under to walk through dirty snowdrifts to school after

how she sat in class knuckles of her left hand rapped by the nuns'
wooden rulers each and every day we imagine her unlearning

each of her inner-most truths this way her the oldest girl of what
would become eight washing dishes four meals a day during

harvest only five years old standing on a stool to reach the farm
sink   we imagine her named by her father this unique this

ostentatious name she could not hide behind imagine learning in
our 20's it was the name of the first woman her father dated the

one that got away the one before he met and married her mother
we would wonder if she was ever loved   by him at night

we imagine Ardell Rose the blonde the oldest girl who I so nearly
resemble her first daughter the one she hates   almost as much

she wiggles her toes

she scrunches them
into the velvet

into the powder
of dark grey dirt

squats down curious
hunches over to touch

hands sifting
fine layers

scritching now with
a bent tablespoon

to the almost packed
earth underneath

crumbling easy
pours itself all back

down the sides into
the hole she made

wondering how it
heals its own wounds

we set out to find the warm red like shame blooming
in hives

the selfsame blood thrum of deep orange in your ear
as sunlight burning through flesh edges

as the soft skin of salvia petals the crow had led us to
and their almost smell of mint

along the rusted camel-back trails along hills
cousined to the Sangre de Cristos

where we finally let the heft of the body nestle
into the reaching shoulders of the earthen crevices

where the lanky stalks of red flowers grew   where we
wept the last of the water and guessed our way back to camp

one part had set out for a transfusion the others wandered
distracted by omens and relics of the mother as if she hadn't

hoarded herself only she could want that's all there was room for
only she could breathe easy

left hand asks rabbit for the story
the source the black humus of clotted blood

right hand tests the glucose finds it low   too low
one more indicator of never enough

a small part remembers mother getting ready mornings
wearing only pantyhose and a tampon

dark legs   dark pooch
a faun   of sorts

white almost everything else blonde hair bleached pale as skin
teased and sprayed big as her ribcage nipples the same

raspberry smear of her rouge empty eyes tangle of dark hair
below parted by the seam by one stray white string

the body makes a rabbit pose it has always known

how to breathe into tight spaces

into discomfort

to make room between the vertebrae to hide

I tell rabbit I want to know where the scars come from
don't I have a right to know

the body opens and twists the legs into deer pose
rests on one still leg that looks to be running

the body shifts it leans on the other leg
this one looks to want to leave

a young a tiny part is riding the back of old stag
eyes closed against the wet-dog gamey thick fur smell of his neck

his eyes either side of his face like rabbit like prey
how we each had been hunted

old stag plays film of us walking in wild grasses taller than me
his wavy pelt velvet and woolen smelling coarse and almost sweet

the body recalls dry hay dusty once-wet cut-grass once-honey
now straw strewn in clumps along a petting zoo

a make-shift lean-to near the pumpkin patch
across from the corn maze and

the particular bustle of feeding quartersfull of tiny hands to
greedy furry lips and how the biggest of them

when all the pellets were gone
stretched out his black tube hose

jizzed on just me

the spider silk spray on my grubby jeans his horizontal eyes
blank with wanting

rain spatters on the metal roof above while I write this then/now
braids synchronicity of sounds threaded throughout the timelines

it speckles and spits each drop a meteor threaded on a comet tail
their fibers spin and web and gather into accordion pleats of time

the girl's eyes glance up to the tall ceiling in that pretty house so
long ago and then fall back down to the white rug

that mother had to have   spread in front of the brick fireplace
flotaki mom had called it   *expensive* dad explained

this was before the divorce when they still had credit this was
when the body was six what did it know other than this smell

this feeling
how we imagined real fur to be

little wing

when we first met the beach my timid sister and I

we were meant to revel in it
this our pretty mother's gift to us upon our uprooting

once we dared
we whooped it up

we staggered in the whorling eddies around our legs and leapt in
were tumbled to our near deaths in the very first swell

her pinkbear mute and rubbed raw

when the ink runs out of the last pen she presses harder along
each letter to at least inscribe the names of the guardians onto

the narrow strips of fortunes she'd collected one cookie at a
time. she coils each one into a tight scroll squeezes it through the

necks of tiny vials she corks them up and places them just so
in the space the broken music box once held she hand stitches

him back to rights and fashions a vest-back out of a thrift store tie
with clashing stripes she patches his empty eye sockets with off-

white scraps from gramma's bag so dapper with his repurposed
braided-leather suit button eyes even a matching tie with what

was left his ratty faded fur a handsome quirk of time. the girl
imagines the little me humming along to his old plinking metal-

comb-and-spool melody as an infant a toddler a girl like herself
hopes that the ululating wavelets of her efforts /now/ would feed

through reverse-osmosis what the little me needed most recalls a
photo of the two of them sharing a white wicker bassinet

everything new and fuzzy them both the same size her folded legs
like chicken wings poking from beneath cloth diapers her little fist

around his back as if comforting him hundreds of years ago
if only the girl could remember what song came after the

creaking squawk of the metal wind-up key but the
feral noises of the past are lost to her were left to

forage to fend for themselves to wander the body
bereft the comforting lapse of space or time.

it feels like love wearing another body

or living fully in your own I suppose it is all the same thing
rabbit's is raw and squishy candy colors and taffy and wet

and womb-like
I imagine the raw warmth of blood

throbbing tissues ligamented to the limestone of porous bone
pockets of tubes and globs and pouches

fractures and repairs and everything trying to hold the rest of it up
colonies of polyps and flagella   connectors   and   unhingers

and tiny floaty things feeding and draining   all hidden
underneath

as we exhale we press and compress the center
with a spiraled puckering

and as we inhale   an unpuckering at the navel
enlarging the body cavity sending breath

to the places that want embodied
to wake them from the past and its flattened sheathes

we breathe into the spine like a straw and lean deep into
the openness we settle into the heels of our feet and wait here

in orbit around an aware body

we find twitches and tics and thumpings in the face and
breathe the tears up to the surface

send those parts beams of pulsing light
feel feral gentling

scan the body again sudden jerk under a shoulder blade
strong tugs at the back we unearth a sisterhood a clamor of voices

all question marks of doubt we breath into as many as we can
witnessing   offering them all of the yesses and thankyous and

we are all okay   now   and I quiver in their company
tell them   *I have missed you*

eyelashes flutter a memory of fist contact
stuttery breaths confirm it

we settle into our body again spread the shoulders
low and wide the upper lip   the warmth of breath

ankles want to run away I uncross them feet flat on the floor
feel toes uncurl

humid is building at the bottom of our left lung
forehead heavy and blink and relax the furrows

I tell the pains

I will try to learn
all of your names

her mother had arranged by phone for her to walk to
the rectory and make herself useful

every week when the 14-year-old arrived the monsignor would
have to come up with things for her to do he had the girl iron

his golf pants or hang towels on the line or take them down if
they were dry or empty the compactor if it was full or use the

cannister vacuum to sweep the thinly lined carpeted floors he
showed her how to clean the birdcage and to replace its lining

from the stack of newspapers near the lanai without spilling she
would carefully finish one task and then go look for him he was

often startled to notice her standing nearby silent and so still
waiting on him to finish whatever he was doing before casting

her eyes downward before asking him what he would like for her
to do next and on the last Thursday of the summer as she was

getting ready to leave he asked her what sins she could possibly
have been atoning for he had always seemed kindly he probably

wanted to offer her forgiveness some form of indulgence for this
quiet little bird of a girl her face went blank she wavered for a bit

and sighing said *there always seems to be something* and turned
away from him to step into the harsh afternoon sun her feet flip-

flopping in time the full six blocks to her mother's stucco condo
which anyone else could see

was ever-so-slowly being swallowed
by the shady maw of an ancient banyan tree

ballad of the bonesetters

i. in which we find him

bird songs outline the ribs of sky
whole villages of warbling banter

of wings scud-tish and skirt along the surfaces of air
as fast as fleet as arrows overhead

while we with legs
we threaded our bodies

thru deer paths thru stickers & seed-heads
clotting up the cowlick-parted grasses ahead

to the chalky clearing
where a skeleton lay

unspooling its sun-bleached bones
knots and dashes splintering along its grain

ii. in which we face him

antlers shooting pirouettes
from knobbled holsters

tufts of fur up like strays of my son's
that once I'd have finger combed flat

eyebrow-lifted expression laced with jagged hems
holes where the tear ducts would have been

this dry-fit assemblage of boney plates
a sacred ruin of architecture

it was the musculature
that did his verbing

teeth still fisted-knuckles open to air
a vining sprig of burgundy leaves as tongue

iii. in which we reckon with a presence

bird bones are light & hollow to help with liftoff
their cellular structure is strong and dense their

hollow vertebrae house lung sacs they pump air
back and forward with each flap each wing beat

it takes that much oxygen that much effort to dis
-rupt gravity this is how I first met little wing   by

breathing deep into my spine hollows   in stretch
-ing forward   to float above my left knee every

exhale a little closer to the broken parts   the
seams   the results of six surgeries a titanium

knee and a commitment that this leg will not
be left behind   the way diabetes and denial

and enough time   took my grandfather's legs
and my dad's

she tells me her name and I whisper it back
we hold us as tight as we can

iv. in which we reckon with an absence

the way she can't quite get a grasp on old stag
who lived in the gap   where the words would

have been
his striding over and forward to defend his land

her body remembers bracing for impact
the purple black sinking and crumpling

and then
and later

the hardening
of scars

today and/or me

she writes and/or metaphors and/or manifests and/or resonates
and/or circles and/or recycles and/or pulses and/or ebbs and/or

vacillates back and/or forth between times and/or addresses

and/or when this today-me (that is, I and/or she) breathes into
and/or waits to know and/ or intuits and/or trowels and/or sifts

for something true and/or writes about it and/or of them
and/or her and/or ourselves and/or her/our parts and/or these

fragmentednesses and/or holds them out for display and/or
validation and/or ridicule and/or for saying a thing out loud

in case it makes it real…

when/then the she/we/now names these parts within the
she/me/we/us that we see/find today

that is also naming it within the them/us from the then/there

and then and/or when now-she and/or et al writes and/or
metaphors and/or et cetera's those parts

which new-me/she/we couldn't have sensed and/or named
and/or even recognized in the then/there

it actually et cetera's those names back to little me and/or us who
is probably staying up past her/our bedtime anyway hiding and/or

listening this provides an introduction at least and/or plants some
seeds in the then/there so et al has them when they/she/we need

them and the royal we all know she/we will need every piece
and/or part we & company can get our collective hands on

and every time and/or address that we/she/us finds
and/or breathes into and/or ad nauseam   more disowned and/or

dissociated parts and/or selves more of them and/or we
are then/now unculled into existence

and future me/we/she can etc all we have ad nauseamed
to the then/there again (before)

and when/then all those little usses grow up and/or in
who knows how whole of a future we might and/or be

who can tell what we might had/have been

the vulture girl wasn't born a bird

but she did begin life   like all of us

an egg   she began this all   as one

smol egg and split into two   she

was not the vulture girl   not yet

she was only twins   just the two

perfectly   mirrored   bodies who

shared the sacred sac   in which

they were wrapped   they shared

it all but shared it   slant   the one

who would   become the vulture

girl outpaced the one   who   would

not   and the one who would not

became   stillness   herself

became silent [fetid] death   and

the   one   who   would   become

a vulture girl   the one who set

her breath by their hearts'   beat

who would never harm her   only

twin did what only a   scavenger

is there   to do   the vulture girl

becomes   the vulture girl   as she

breathes in   her sister cells   her

other selves   she purifies   the

charnel   grounds   of this one's

womb   the other one's tomb

a small imprint   on the left foot

of the little wing   she lived with

and the   little wing   she died

alongside   a birthmark   marker

for bodies lost and won   a wing

span   that could have circled

and circled and circled   the sun

the whirlpool in her belly

she counts the tzeet-churk tzeet-churk heartbeat cricket bleating
her pulse in the neck she counts the brackish ebbs

of the brine eddies unsteadying her count she counts anything
else to ignore the thirst the parched the arid flakes of dryness on

every soft-tissued edge squelched together rubber and stiff from
wanting she clenches   she   exhales to exhale even harder

until she has no   spaces   left   and   collapses
into a wheezing an avalanching whistle of inlet

a cyclonic black hole suck of an eye streaming with the shame
the daring   of needing   of taking   a breath

the sting of saltwater torrents invading every   place   even
those she didn't know   she had   she begs the universe for less

but it   won't quit
she barely bears it her body all bladder how she grits to contain it

the blames of searing stretching fish-stink depths
how she sinks and floats she buoys the tides and holds and holds

and holds and
holds too much   she is out of   hands   it is   as if

her   ears
grow   further   and   further   apart

the cricketing is slower is spreading is widening its quaver
its tenoring creak is bellowing   basser

a deflating hiss a sonorous a sloshing a resounding eructating spill
of bilic dirge of irascible of melancholic purge

these scarce moments between   she can't even mouth her pleas
how she was trying to please how she concedes she ate the fruit

so now she bleeds either pregnant or cramps is all she was built
for what else could a wench like her ever wish for

there were bruises like grapes on her forearms

I don't care if he did
get you those fake credit cards

the girl told her mother
you said we moved here

to get away
from all of that

you can't blame the stone for its strength

in the tornado dreams she never had time to feel scared
those parts if they ran fast enough always land on their feet

find themselves deep in wall's keep but the parts that were
curious the parts that she is mostly

the parts that want the choice even when they ask nicely and had
all been well-behaved if they arranged

the body into legs against the wall pose to honor to placate to
submit and when they ask to meet it gently   even   when they beg

wall
blocks them all

is intellect and bone is arthritic stone is gristly
avoidance an impenetrable a thing unto itself

is always
has always been

had stood like this
for all her years

until she doodled a stone enclosure and fitted a black iron handle
sometimes the wall is also a door she says & draws a keyhole too

she begins to feel her way in   her hands
reach ahead of her in the dark starlight of mind

a murmur of tiny eyelid twitching an almost nostril flare here
is the first smallishness that had ever required wall's strength

her refuge
her cage

and once recognized   this young part rises
free to swim in the warm ocean of the body

it leads her to stairs to a narrow column of Jenga blocks a stack
of bulging discs she clambers up onto in the coolness the damp

she finds the idea of wall in the root cellar smells of old wood and
rain in thick slabs of stone finding shelter in abandoned homes

she can hear wall deep within her skull cave
earthen floors worn smooth with pacing she

conjures an image of him sitting there like a regular person
feet up on an old steamer trunk he uses for a coffee table

she is here   she says   to re-negotiate wall's contract   suggests
he might like to retire soon   have more time to travel   he

agrees   he signs the paperwork   hands over the schematics
he explains the workings of the wishbone latch at the throat

the one he uses to shut out the dirty rabble of loud and unruly
she nods appreciative and leaves   follows the long pathway of

the trachea reaches her thin fingers into the bottle of her neck
and reverses the clasp

vulture

you need a spanking

she whispered her yelling
still twanging my ears

she doesn't care that I am on my period
she says   she waits

while I take off the second-hand pants
waistband folded three times over

and stained underwear
soggy pad queasy in it

lay them on the bed
near the stick on the covers

where I lay my head
and bend over

before the eclipse when he allows her in

the night pulsing purple through bare trees
painted with the gleaming char of the moon

not yet bleeding as foretold but
brittle and porous as bone

she falls into a world of wooden gymnasium bleachers
set up just along the edge of a dry-stacked shale wall

built in the olden times outlining a steep granite ravine
of a dried up river bed littered with autumn leaves

like wadded paper bags   whole families chattering
birdlike in the stands   disinterested in the marvel

of the feral the speckled and piebald horses clattering
and shuttling past in fits and starts all stout and thick

in their winter coats with mismatched manes

she walks back to her seat but stag has taken her place
shifts his upright body aside as if to make room

she settles awkward along his breathing flank
against the bulk of his chest   his antlers askance

the wood grain of coarse hairs at his sternum   imagines
how the weight might feel to walk centered so far forward

stag reaches his left foreleg elbow up along
her shoulder at the back of her neck

his shank following the base of her skull
and drapes his ankle his shin his hooves

over her crown   onto her forehead
the third eye   this embrace   a sacred clasp

he lowers the chin of his noble head and
from his smooth dark nostrils   he huffs

he chuffs warmly onto her hair   kindly
he presses his breath deep into her scalp

she inhales through her pores his musky
protection   shudders inside his fur along her spine

she breathes through his lungs
into the xylophone of his rib cage

the coil of his rump and springs
the wax wood cage around his head

the thick eyelashes circling
his blank mercury eyes

Spring Hill KS, 1978

she goes to cartwheel in the yard limbs like wagon-wheel-spokes
belly a hub of extremities first legs then arms straight and leaning

leaning for momentum she overturns the girl she pinwheels
across the lawn the quick ung-ung ung-ung of bare feet in

damp dirt   of bare hands in long grass a kiss on each cheek of
earth to push off from   hair akimbo stretching all up spinning

she has become her own planet   tumbleweeding an orbit the
size of her reach   slowly slowing down   the song of a wobbly

quarter tilting inward lilting keeling into a stuttered staccato
shuddering   uncartwheelish   and   stopped

yet another of those
jarred-into silences

wide eyes listen for the bloodrush to swirl less roary less thumpy
in the summer-sun that staggers soft-focused hexagonal pixels

down the jagged limbs above to flatten the jangled weeds back
down into the horizon she tests the air with a bent elbow in case

gravity allows it   then shoulders up head heavy and askew a
ragged banjo-laugh chords from the mouth as she attempts to

stand and is slapped flat rubberband back
like *heaviness* dressed up as an active verb

almost invisible an airplane drills a tiny white scratch in the blue
flies buzzing leaving highlighter scribbles aurora-like overhead she

is distracted by their hum by the clack of dishes being washed in
the sink next door the body is staggering is twisting is up already

spiraling spry in the way of seven-year-olds   tenacious in the way
of weary necessity   her summersaults every crash every dare

feedback she creates the conditions of
every scar   proof   she lived through the scare

thermogenesis of flight

what if I told you that we who house tornadoes within we who
walk the earth in whispers because we don't want to wake the

thundering clatterers what if you knew   we could let it go could
dissipate the energy through the production of heat

you may not believe it but I trust when intensity makes my
eyebrows sweat   that some healing has occurred what if

we could secrete hurt like steam   raising thermals from our
warmth   launched to the heights where it could cool

where water vapors aggregate where they form cumulus clouds
and descend back to the ground the pain pattering like rain

like the slow flit of feathers
settling into bird shape again

fawning

she builds the fawn around her of sticks felled in the brisk winds
from the old cottonwood each limb barkless creamy smooth each

set of legs set at a skittish an awkward angle the girl fashions a
hide of worn-thin chicken-wire wrapped round her sharpest

corners and plied in layers of papier-mache pulped from the
scrapbook pages grandma made for him handwritten captions in

that square & even cursive for her first born that first year before
the first set of twins stiff photo squares pulling off from their dark

yellow tape moorings brown newsprint toasted with time and
deckled at the edges with neglect she coos softly almost purrs

to herself as she works the paste into the paper strips into the
spaces still left or torn open into whatever else will hide her

from this cage of her own making she weaves a small broom of
her old stitches and sweeps up the bottle caps, shards of plastic,

stripped cigarette filters, walnut hulls, pebbles, and metal springs
left behind she makes a bedding of it she tucks her cold feet up

into her layers as the fawn is marionetted about is buffeted on
the prevailing whims of others   she is lulled into a sort of slumber

by the erratic rocking by the loving knocking by the goings on
outside of her pinata skin

exigency of the vulture

what if you told me that you could fly in a spiraling circular path
within these columns of air and survive the aftereffects of my

trauma of the cloying smothering of self that I suffer that these
eddies these currents could be ridden to higher and higher

altitudes what if you meant "me" when you said "you" and what if
we went together both of us vultures weighing very little

two maybe three pounds our slightness lets us glide into the sky
into the off-gassing of my of all of our internal dangers our arms

outspread wide and carefree the occasional twitchy tilt as we
fractal up in the opposite of a free-fall the concentration of our

mass not in these broad wingspans or the mechanicals required to
hurl ourselves skyward but in the clump of viscera underneath in

the sack of liquids that run our engines held pinioned aloft
between the wire-winged armature of our turkey buzzard flight

our white gray feathers from beneath
gone silver as they catch the light

I wanted to see rabbit again

her image insubstantial of late but   *that is the nature*
of metaphors   rabbit shrugged   so I asked if I could feel

her instead and she gurgled in my stomach from her warren right
as the dog's elbow smushed into my lips   like a furry rabbit kiss

he'd never gone under the bed before   this dog   his awkward
army-crawl noises so strange and distracting that I had joined him

laying on my belly   breathing deeply while asking myself to see an
imaginary rabbit and now I'm three or four again

laying on the floor having wet the bed in the cold dawn of an
easter morning hiding underneath so I won't get into trouble

arms folded under my chin my head snuggled into my elbow
just like our body is now and we're telling myself it's

okay it might dry out before anyone wakes up
thinking I might see the easter bunny in the act from here

and as I fall asleep waiting that's when rabbit first wakes up
this is her posture she reassures me

body will always be able to find her this way

fawn

bicephaly among feral Cervidae: a case study

the mother gave birth to two fawns pretty little things she'd pull
us from her pocket occasionally

so we could
perform for her friends

mother bore two fawns most does give birth to twins it is a reflex
to lie   coiled up and flat

to lie still   to depend on not attracting
unwanted attention

this fawn had two   perfect fawn heads
on two perfectly articulated necks and

two lungs that never once breathed
air into its one small pouch of a body

two small hearts in one
shared sac like twins in

one
womb

they call it fawning when the body can't tell where the edges are
when it doesn't even sense enough of its self to emit its own smell

that day on the forest floor their mottled
sunflecked fur all new and deftly groomed

\unviable\

cleaned with a mother's tongue no doubt
asking

/please/

teats full and lingering absolutions
but   still   they would not stir

the two headed fawn (she/they) could barely fill my cupped hands
mouth parts already parted preparing to nuzzle

the doe stayed longer than was safe till spooked
by the footsteps of the mushroom hunter

had been inhaling their scentlessness   reluctant to
leave the fawnlings

as their body cooled   in the
chill outside   her body

it is a reflex
dropping to the ground at the first sign of danger

to collapse your rickety legs too weak yet to outrun the hunter
you were given to by your mother

even a shiver
the slightest flinch

could give you away

in other words   they were that pair of
fledgling birds found on a needled bed

lying noiseless in the shadow of the dark pine
on the same morning as a friend's miscarriage

her two perfect boys' flightless wings
raised high around each other's heads

embracing

in one time that she did cross
that threshold alert and suckling

she grew twice as large since
she could feed   twice as fast

the fawn became a strong doe
herself bearing generations of

two-headed deer her two-headed
stag sons   antlered like the gods

or she barely survived it and
remained freckled and puny

she found with her keen acuity
(observing in all four directions)

she could alert the herd faster
learned to make herself useful

so the others
tolerated her

and every time she was born alive
they shared their sister thoughts

with each
other

in the way that each fish in
a school has a whole organ

devoted to where the
rest of them are

and those times that the fawn died
her lungs   being too compressed in

their joiningness
to inflate

at least she left certain
in her completeness in

their entangled connectedness
w/anything they could possibly

experience
or imagine

the girl thinks of how stag passed away without sharing his/
her secrets

so as to prevent their
crushing her

she decided that stag might have been
or that   maybe   she even was   that

stillborn fawn
all along

shut down and dreaming
of a noble guardianship

in that timelessness that will
occur in the hallucinations of

any vaguely living thing at its end
casting thin strands of timelines

grasping
and

gasping
like

land-stranded fish
unable to wrest enough oxygen

from the air

tornado

how the vulture lost its voice

vulture has no melody or mimicry
unlike the songbirds who take full

advantage of their voice box their
syrinx   making several sounds in

and out   an organ   evolved from
the dinosaur   while they still had

a functioning larynx as well it's a
mystery as to why or how   and in

all this abundance   the buzzard
benefits from neither   the syrinx

which she does not have   nor the
larynx which for her has no vocal

folds   no sound at all forged from
the trachea   to where   it forks

into the lungs   she can only hiss
and grunt   and   maybe wheeze

the turkey vulture *Cathartesx aura*
which means   *purifying   breeze*

in early spring after the wasp nest was cleared from the swing set
having already been stung once the vulture girl climbed to its

tippy-top wrapped her arms around the cool hollow metal tube
and would warble the softest high-pitched syllables into the ether

her voice like ancient tuning reeds as the sun slanted brightly
through the bare trees this wordlessness scarcely breathed so

wall wouldn't know she sang she came gently unbound
until the sniffling made it hard to make any other sound

before it was known as the wishbone
the furcula was called a *merrythought*

and believed to grant a wish to the holder
of the larger end of it when pulled apart

before then   the bone was used in the
prediction of upcoming storms

that process has been lost to antiquity

the tornados would chase her in her dreams as if they could seek
her out   were sentient were teasing her their gyrating columns of

terror skittering to the foreground and then faltering away whole
families of them spiraling to earth all at once these storm systems

and their greedy scrabbling their destructive clawing fingers
colonizing the turbulent skies and she would hear the sirens

would urge the people around her to run to safety to get into
their root cellars to keep behind wall like she was always doing

the word *furcula* means little fork it makes
us think of tuning forks of pitch/ forks and

resonance it is a fusion of their clavicles it
strengthens the thorax to withstand flight

acts like a spring between the shoulders
storing the energy of the upstroke

as it expands
then contracts in a snap

to pull the wings down filling the body with
air at every wingbeat holding its breath

as it glides

it wasn't until she would wake up when she would recall that
the tornado's open maw was roaring and churning inside of her

regardless whenever she closes her eyes or is still for too long
always a whirling cesspool heaving inward and inward and her

looking down into the verge of its bottomlessness that she has
always been just on the brink of

                              she felt as if she might have to break
                              herself open if she was ever going

                              to make herself whole to dig herself out
                              with her own gottdamn fork

                              tear herself apart by the collarbones and
                              give one half to someone to anyone else

                              and pull with all of her gizzard grit
                              that this time   might be different

this
vulture

body
seeks the sun

stretches up raises its wings open elbows pulled back and scrapes
the scapulae together lifting and lowering to massage the spine

it reaches arms high hands clasped and arches her back again
lets the neck open to the sun-star lifting its beak swiveling

the back of her bald head against the fat of her shoulder hump
slowly blinks its nictating membranes and exposes

each ear hole to the warmth to the cleansing heat of sun
she solemnly bows forward tail feathers spread

and resets
shaking everything loose

feathers aerated
like empty pinecones

there.
she has

paid her
respects

now
she must feed

still the girl dreamt of cyclones menacing and thick with debris
pocked with flocks of Victorian-styled shoes perforated and pointy

always she'd be huddled behind damp cinder blocks   blood
thumping in her ears as aboveground they hunted her it wouldn't

be long until she would try to swallow the tornado itself whole by
the handsfull until she would empty the bottle of pills until dusty

powder residue was all that was left until she finally slept without
dreaming until some of that tornado seeped out through the

black velvet of activated charcoal swirling up her esophagus like
bats swarming at sundown a cotton batting a tinnitussive silence

until the rotation of hot magma returned now with metallic
harmonics now pushing her toward the hurtling stench

of its grasp   until wall engineered that   wishbone latch

the poor were often proffered bread and
mead or wine to be eaten over a corpse

an exchange that counted the sins of the
departed toward the damnation of the fed

an absolution of guilt for those who could
afford it and a reverse last supper for the

sin-eaters who were regarded as unclean
who had to keep a respectful distance

the reason for that stance the *horaltic pose*
with her wings raised high and flapping

in the sun is for the bird to disinfect her
self in the heat to cleanse to rid herself

of whatever her own piss or vomit hadn't
the root word refers to a dance in Hebrew

the way we all circle like steam
from a kettle across the heavens

in Sanskrit it indicated a form of astrology
of predicting the future

stretching so high as if to peek
over the horizon of time.

feeling a
little less

untethered than usual   vulture girl   now an old woman
wondered   if her trauma were not a tornado anymore at all

but a funnel cloud-shaped   murmuration   of streaming vultures
having fed off it until there was none

peppering the sky with their dance
spreading pieces of it throughout all the expanse

of the infinite prairie summer skies
diluting it

and
then

airing it out to dry
purifying it

in the heat
of the

clean white
paper sun

in gratitude

vulture girl was a labor of love and self-reclamation.
special thanks to the collective of guardians and guides who've
gotten me/us this far...

to the Sundress Academy of the Arts, to Erin Elizabeth Smith and
Firefly Farms for the generous hospitality of the Writer's Coop
year after year, for the sweet cabin where so much of this all
began and where I sat at last with a completed draft...

and the Community of Writers Virtual Valley 2021 for the model
of gracious support, for the time, space, craft talks, and sense of
community; eight poems were wrenched out of me that week
and most are in this book. A huge THANK YOU to Kazim Ali
whose belief in my writing enabled that opportunity in the first
place...

to Peggy Dobreer and her Slow Lightning meditation/writing
group whose imagery during CoW helped extract the poems
"you can't blame stone for its strength" and "207 W Allen"...

to Jeanine Oulette and Elephant Rock whose online classes are
inspiration for the soul and nourishment for my writing practice;
and specifically, where the poem "wall arrives too late" was first
conceived...

to Gillian, a steadfast friend and fellow poet/artist and AROHO
alum, thank you for your kind and heartfelt presence from clear
across the globe...

to Janett for your faith in me and for sharing your family and your
heart...

to Em for their lovely patience and caring in offering the time for that impromptu (and overly long) reading when this book first began to feel real…

and to all the little me's, may you truly know that you are love(d).

notes

Much of the poem, "bicephaly among feral Cervidae: a case study" is owed to the original study and photos by D'Angelo et al at the University of Georgia which published in the journal, *American Midland Naturalis,* (accessed online); in which a man foraging for mushrooms came across a two-headed fawn shortly after it must have been born and had the forethought to preserve it for science. Bicephaly is rare in domesticated animals, but rarer still in the wild.

And "the whirlpool in her belly" was adapted from the ancient story of Charybdis who helped her father, Poseidon, to flood the land. She was punished for it by her uncle, Zeus, who gave her an unquenchable thirst for salt water. She personified the (not actually that) treacherous whirlpool in the Messina Strait along with (possibly her daughter) Scylla, who represented a rocky shoal on the opposite side. Scylla had been changed into a six-headed, sailor-eating monster due to the jealousy of Amphrite and/or Circe. The two she-monsters were thought to menace the narrow seaway since Odysseus' times and became the original "rock and hard place" aphorism of ancient Greece. The irony is that, while navigating the strait could be dangerous, being female clearly had much less margin for error.

acknowledgments

The Comstock Review: "yesterday the gods told me to fall into my own eyes"

Concision Poetry Journal: "today and/or me"

FERAL: "she first saw old stag several years before they'd met"

Quartet: "the vulture girl wasn't born a bird"
& nominated for Best of the Net 2023

Written Here and There: The Community of Writers Poetry Review, 2021: "207 W Allen"

resources

Anodea Judith's *Chakra Yoga* has been instrumental in preparing the body to listen before it could write. It is a generous and gentle introduction to yoga poses, the meaning of the chakras, and to developing a personal yoga practice.

Lewis Mehl-Madrona's book *Coyote Wisdom: The Power of Story in Healing* (and his presentation at the Creativity and Madness conference in Santa Fe, NM many years ago) provided a template for accessing the inner guide(s) waiting for me all along.

Richard C. Schwartz' book, *No Bad Parts: Healing Trauma & Restoring Wholeness with The Internal Family Systems Model* is an excellent resource for addressing our multiple internal parts.

about Carrie Nassif

Carrie Nassif (she/hers) is a queer poet, photographer, clinical psychologist, and creativity coach living outside of Taos, NM.

Her first collection, *lithopeadion,* was a featured book in SAFTA's Wardrobe's Best Dressed and a finalist in Yes Yes Book's Vinyl 45 Chapbook Contest.

Recent poetry can be found in *The Comstock Review, Concision Poetry Journal, FERAL, Quartet,* and several anthologies; she also has poetry book reviews with *Colorado Review* and *Birch Bark Editing.*

More information is available at carrienassifphd.com/author.